America's
Wetlands

America's
Wetlands

A Carolrhoda Earth Watch Book

written and photographed by Frank Staub

Carolrhoda Books, Inc./Minneapolis

For Bob, Martha, and Chelsea

Additional photograph p. 38 courtesy of the Irish Tourist Board

Carolrhoda Books, Inc., c/o The Lerner Group
241 First Avenue North, Minneapolis, MN 55401

LIBRARY OF CONGRESS CATALOGING-IN-PUBLICATION DATA

Staub, Frank J.
America's wetlands / written and photographed by Frank Staub.
p. cm.
Includes index.
ISBN 0-87614-827-5
1. Wetlands—North America—Juvenile literature. 2. Wetland ecology—North America—Juvenile literature. [1. Wetlands. 2. Wetland ecology. 3. Ecology.] I. Title.
QH102.S737 1995
574.5'26325'097—dc20
94-3872
CIP
AC

Manufactured in the United States of America

1 2 3 4 5 6 – I/JR – 00 99 98 97 96 95

CONTENTS

Vanishing Nurseries   7

Recognizing a Wetland   11

Water and Grass   16

Wetlands That Aren't Always Wet   19

Between the Land and the Sea   24

Nature's High Energy Factories   30

Storing Energy—The Peatlands   34

Keepers of the Land's Water   39

No Net Loss   42

Glossary   46

Index   47

About the Author   48

VANISHING NURSERIES

Not long ago, a flock of ducks had a terrible surprise. They had just flown a thousand miles northward up the middle of North America. It was breeding time, and they were looking for a place to build their nests and lay their eggs. But the pothole pond where they had nested in the past was gone.

For thousands of years, most of the ducks between the Mississippi River and the Rocky Mountains have raised their young along the shores of small ponds called prairie potholes. These shallow patches of water dot the dry plains of the northern United States and Canada. Their edges are thick with grass where the young birds can find food and hide from enemies. Prairie potholes are **habitats** that the ducks cannot live without. A habitat is an environment in which animals live and breed. Once there were thousands of prairie pothole habitats. Now half are gone because farmers drained them to grow crops.

The tired ducks kept on flying. Eventually, they did find a prairie pothole. But hundreds of other ducks had found it too, and the nesting spots had all been taken. So the ducks that had just arrived didn't get to have any young that year. With the loss of so much habitat, there aren't nearly as many ducks as there used to be.

Toads mating in a temporary forest pond in Rhode Island

Toads living in a New England forest had a similar problem. Unlike birds, toads must lay their eggs underwater. Otherwise, the jelly-like eggs will dry out. One place where these toads had always found water was in a pond that appeared briefly in the forest after the spring rains. But the people in a nearby town who owned the forest decided to dump rocks and gravel in the low area where the little pond formed. Then they covered it with asphalt to make a parking lot.

When spring came, the toads looked for other wet places to lay their eggs. Some tried to cross the parking lot. Many didn't make it to the other side. Those that did never found any water. Today there are very few toads living in that forest. In fact, the number of toads, frogs, and other amphibians has dropped all over the world, partly because of habitat loss.

Like the midwestern ducks and the New England toads, the fishermen in Louisiana have known some hard times. The fish they catch grow up among the grasses in the shallow, salty waters along the coast. These areas are called salt marshes. But oil wells, boat channels, and other structures have replaced many of Louisiana's salt marshes. As a result, there are fewer fish to catch, and some of the fishermen have had trouble making enough money to support their families.

Salt marshes, prairie potholes, and temporary forest ponds are three kinds of wetlands. There are many other wetland types in North America, such as freshwater marshes, swamps, bogs, fens, wet meadows, vernal pools, washes, mudflats, and riparian areas. Unlike dry land, the dominant feature in a wetland environment is water.

As wetlands become more scarce, some Louisiana fishermen are finding it hard to catch fish.

Any low point in the land that collects water may support a wetland. The edges of streams, lakes, and rivers are good places to find wetlands. Even the ditches that humans dig to carry water to our crops and away from our highways support plants and animals that survive only in places where water is abundant for at least part of the year.

Wetlands cover just 6 percent of the earth's total land area. Yet they are among the earth's liveliest places. More animals depend on wetlands than on practically any other natural habitat except the ocean. Three-quarters of our bird species, most of the fish and shellfish we eat, and many of our mammals, reptiles, and amphibians spend at least part of their lives in or very near wetlands. The reason is simple: all life needs water. Water is the most abundant chemical in the bodies of all living things. Plants need it to grow. And animals not only drink water, they also find food, make homes, have young, and play either in water or next to it.

A wide variety of animals, including the great egret and its snake prey at left and the moorhen and nutria shown above, depend on wetlands.

Even some drainage ditches beside railroad tracks and highways can be called wetlands.

RECOGNIZING A WETLAND

Obviously, a wetland is wet. But how wet? And for how long a time must a place be wet to be called a wetland? Different people have different answers for these questions.

Some scientists refer to any body of water except rain puddles and the sea as a wetland. Others differentiate between wetlands and deepwater environments. A deepwater environment is any part of a river, lake, or ocean where the water is deeper than six feet. Unlike many of the plants and animals in wetlands, deepwater life forms never contact the air.

One thing scientists look for in a wetland are water-loving plants called **hydrophytes.** The word *hydrophyte* comes from the Greek words for water *(hydro-)* and plant *(-phyte)*. Not all wetlands have hydrophytes, but if hydrophytes are present, an area is definitely a wetland. Hydrophytes must grow in soil that is waterlogged or saturated at some point during the year. Saturated soil contains so much water that it can't hold any more. A place may appear dry, but if hydrophytes grow there, the soil is or has been saturated.

American lotus, a hydrophyte, growing in a marsh

Algae growing on a lake surface. If algae grows too thick, it may use up all the water's oxygen, leaving none for animals living in the water.

Most hydrophytes have roots, stems, and leaves, just like the plants we usually see. Wetlands also contain hydrophytes that don't have roots, stems, or leaves. These are the algae. Some algae are made up of just one cell and cannot be seen without a microscope. Algae cells often float freely in the water. But sometimes the tiny algae cells join together to form a slippery green skin on the bottom mud, the surfaces of larger plants, or even on the water's surface.

Hydrophytes may fill a wetland from one end to the other. But according to some scientists, an area doesn't have to have any plants at all to be called a wetland, as long as water is abundant from time to time. This means that the beaches of rocks, sand, and gravel splashed by waves from lakes and oceans are also wetlands.

Below: *A moose takes advantage of a stream.* Right: *Cormorants roost in cypress trees in a swamp.*

The two most common kinds of wetlands are freshwater marshes and swamps. Both are covered by a shallow layer of water for most, if not all, of the year. Turtles, frogs, birds, bobcats, moose, rabbits, deer, raccoons, snakes, alligators, salamanders, and many other animals may be found in both marshes and swamps.

A swamp and a marsh are not the same, though many people think they are. In a marsh, the most common hydrophyte is grass, or plants that look like grass, such as rushes and sedges. These plants have soft rather than woody stems. Unlike marshes, swamps are dominated by either trees or shrubs. Trees and shrubs contain stiff, woody fibers that support the plant bodies and allow them to grow taller than the soft-bodied plants of the marsh. Swamps generally look like forests with floors of smooth water.

One of the most famous wetlands in the world for seeing birds and other wild animals is Everglades National Park in southern Florida. Like a great river, the water in the Everglades creeps southward across vast grassy plains and around small islands of trees.

Most of the swampland in North America is in the southeast. There the weather is warm, so the trees grow quickly. Also, there's plenty of rain, and there are many low flat areas to collect water.

Many wetlands are either swamp-like or marsh-like. Some wetlands, such as Everglades National Park in southern Florida, are mixtures of swamps, marshes, dry islands, and areas of open water. A small number of swamps and marshes in North America contain salt water. Salt-water wetlands occur in coastal areas where there's plenty of shallow ocean water.

Coots in a cattail marsh. Cattails are one of the most common marsh plants.

WATER AND GRASS

Most of North America's wetlands are freshwater marshes of some kind. Prairie potholes are one example of freshwater marshes. Cattails and bulrushes are the most common hydrophytes in America's freshwater marshes. Scientists call these emergent plants because their tops grow out of, or emerge from, the surface of the water.

Marshes may also contain plants that never grow above the water's surface. These plants are called submergents. The submergent plants in a marsh may be the same species as those in the deepwater environments farther from shore. In addition, marshes contain floating plants. Their leaves float on the water's surface, while their stems are underwater and rooted to the bottom. Water lilies, duckweed, and water hyacinths are examples of floating plants.

Some typical wetland dwellers: a great egret (left), *a swamp rabbit* (above, top), *and red-eared turtles covered with duckweed* (above, bottom)

The abundant marsh plants provide good habitats for fish, birds, and other creatures. In fact, a freshwater marsh is one of the best places on earth to spot interesting animals.

Marsh creatures fit perfectly into a wetland existence. In other words, they have adapted to their environment. Many marsh birds, such as herons and egrets, have long legs for wading and long bills for nabbing fish, snakes, and other marsh dwellers.

Birds that wade in marshes also tend to have wide feet to help them walk on the marsh plants. Even marsh rabbits, and their cousins swamp rabbits, have wide feet for stability.

Freshwater marshes are water-covered most of the time. But when there is little rain, the water level may drop. When this happens, the shallow edge of the marsh may dry out. If the edge of a marsh is dry more often than it is wet, and if the plants growing there are different from those in the wetter parts of the marsh, the marsh edge is called a **wet meadow.** Sedges are often the dominant wet meadow plants. A sedge looks like a grass, but grasses have joints in their stems, while sedges do not. During dry periods, much of the water in the leaves of cattails and other marsh plants passes into the air through evaporation. But sedge plants hold on to their water for a much longer time. As we'll soon see, sedges aren't the only wetland plants that have to deal with dryness.

During dry periods, the edges of a marsh may dry out to become a wet meadow.

Alligators help other wetlands animals by creating "gator holes" during dry periods.

WETLANDS THAT AREN'T ALWAYS WET

Water makes a wetland. But wetlands may, at certain times of the year, have no visible water. Wet meadows are a good example. In addition, about one-fifth of our prairie potholes are dry during part of the year. Likewise, the temporary forest ponds where the New England toads breed lose their water by the end of autumn, as rainfall decreases.

Any wetland may dry up if rainfall is low enough. In many southeastern marshes, alligators help birds, fish, turtles, and other marsh animals survive dry periods by thrashing out holes with their powerful bodies and tails. Water collects in these "gator holes," which quickly become centers for life. If the alligator dies, its hole may be taken over by another alligator. Or the hole may eventually be filled in by plants and disappear.

In the dry plains and deserts of western North America, there is a common wetland that is dry more often than it is wet. It is called a wash. A wash is a stream bed of rocks, sand, or gravel that is covered by water only after heavy rains. The stream of water may remain for weeks, days, or just a few hours, depending on the amount of rainfall. Rainstorms aren't very common in many parts of the West, so washes rarely contain enough water for a stream to develop.

The moisture-loving plants growing beside a wash don't look like the cactus and other desert species on the higher and much drier lands nearby. For that matter, the plants beside almost any stream, lake, or river are often very different from species growing in drier soil farther from the water. The moist environments next to bodies of water are called **riparian areas.**

Riparian plants may be hydrophytes. They may also be **mesophytes,** which are plants that need moist but not saturated soil. No matter what kind of plant a riparian species is, it cannot tolerate dryness as well as nonriparian species.

VERNAL POOLS

When heavy rains come to the farmlands of California's great Central Valley, small ponds called **vernal pools** form. *Vernal* means "of spring," the season when the pools appear. The water in a vernal pool may last a few months or just days. But during that time, up to two hundred kinds of plants grow from seeds that other plants shed the previous spring. The seeds have remained in the dry mud through the summer, fall, and winter.

Vernal pools also contain tiny swimming animals called fairy shrimp, which hatch from eggs buried in the mud. The tiny shrimp are less than 1 inch (2.5 cm) long, with translucent bodies and feathery legs on their bellies for swimming.

After the rain stops, the vernal pools dry up, and the plants and animals they contain die. But their seeds and eggs remain, waiting for the next year's rains.

A desert wash is dry more often than it is wet. The trees growing along the edge of the wash are riparian plants.

Most of the animals in the western United States depend on the riparian areas near rivers and streams.

In the dry southwestern United States, three-quarters of the land's wildlife depend on moist riparian areas. Yet riparian areas in that part of the country make up only two or three percent of the total land surface. The riparian lands in other parts of North America are also limited, and also very important to wildlife.

Some animals live in riparian areas all year long. Others just come in for brief visits to feed or have their young. In North America's forests and plains, the only drinkable water for miles around may trickle down the center of a few small riparian forests and meadows.

Riparian areas may sit next to swamps or marshes. But unlike these two habitats, a riparian wetland has no water above the soil, except when the nearby stream, river, or lake rises above its banks in a flood. Riparian and other low areas that are periodically flooded are called **floodplains**.

Humans fear floods. But floods moisten the soil and make new plant growth possible. As the currents of water spread out across a floodplain, they slow down. The sluggish water no longer has enough energy to carry **sediments,** the small solid particles that make the water look muddy. The sediments gradually fall to the floodplain surface to form soil.

Over the years, soil builds up on a floodplain layer by layer. Floodplain soil is often full of nutrients, the chemicals plants need to grow. Nutrients are minerals, such as potassium, magnesium, calcium, and phosphorus. Nutrient-rich soil and the water from floods are what make plants grow so well on floodplains. People have found floodplains to be among the best places on earth for crops. Indeed, the earliest civilizations developed on the floodplains of great rivers such as the Nile in Africa, the Tigris and Euphrates in the Middle East, and the Indus in Asia.

Floodplains can be dangerous places to build houses.

BETWEEN THE LAND AND THE SEA

One of the hardest places for hydrophytes to survive is the seashore. Ocean waves can injure delicate stems and leaves. When the average hydrophyte is placed in the sea, water flows out of its body and into the surrounding salt water, causing the plant to die.

Another threat to hydrophytes living on the sea coast is the constant rise and fall of the tides. Each day, there are two high tides and two low tides. The area between the highest point reached by the high tides and the lowest point reached by the low tides is a wetland called the intertidal zone. The width of the intertidal zone varies from a few feet to many feet, depending on the location, season, and shape of the coastline.

Sunset on a Mississippi salt marsh. Inset: *Spartina grass, the most common hydrophyte in America's salt marshes, at low tide*

Fish and other water animals swim and crawl across the intertidal zone when the tide is in. Land animals visit the intertidal zone during low tide. Low tide is also the time when those plants and animals that live permanently in the intertidal zone are exposed to the air and risk drying out.

Few wetland plants other than algae can deal with the hazards of intertidal life. One plant that can is a grass with the lovely scientific name *Spartina alterniflora*. Spartina grass is the most common hydrophyte in the great chain of salt marshes that stretches along North America's Atlantic coast from Maine to Florida and Louisiana.

Arrowgrass, a common hydrophyte on the West Coast, is beginning to grow on this mudflat, which will eventually give way to a salt marsh.

Only about five percent of America's wetlands are salt marshes. A salt marsh can develop only in a place that is shielded from the full force of the ocean surf. The most common places to find salt marshes are along the shores of **estuaries.** An estuary is that part of a river that experiences the rise and fall of the ocean tides. It is the river's mouth, where the fresh river water mixes with the salt water of the sea to form brackish water. Brackish water contains less salt than pure sea water, but more salt than fresh water. There are more estuaries and salt marshes on the East Coast of North America than on the West Coast because there are more rivers flowing into the Atlantic Ocean than the Pacific.

A river entering an estuary carries many nutrients washed down from the land in the runoff from rain and melting snow. The nutrients help the salt-marsh plants thrive. Large numbers of fish, birds, and other animals that eat salt-marsh plants owe their survival to the abundance of nutrients.

Estuaries also receive sediments. As the river enters the estuary, it slows down, and any sediments it may be carrying fall to the bottom. The muddy sediments pile up and eventually start to appear above the water's surface as a flat plain of mud called a **mudflat**. Green-colored algae often grow on the surface of a mudflat wetland. Also living both on and in the mud are large numbers of clams, worms, and snails.

As the sediments pile up on a mudflat, the high tides cover the mud for shorter and shorter periods. When the mud is piled high enough, spartina grass takes root. As a spartina plant matures, it sends out underground stems called **rhizomes**, which give rise to new plants. These in turn produce more plants, and eventually a salt marsh is born.

Mudflats at low tide are good places to dig for clams.

Once a salt marsh forms, the mud piles up faster because, as the water flows past the plants, it slows down even more and deposits more sediment. The muddy bottom rises higher and higher until eventually it is hardly ever covered by the tides. Then the hydrophytes die off, and land plants start to move in. In this way, new land is created. The change from mudflat to dry land happens so slowly over the years that no one really notices.

Most wetlands collect sediments and gradually bury themselves just as salt marshes do. But as old wetlands are buried, new wetlands develop along the newly formed shorelines.

Wetland plants are beginning to take over this stretch of beach along the Rio Grande in Texas.

The roots of mangrove trees are strong enough to withstand hurricanes.

Salt marshes are found on coastlines with cold winters. But along the south Florida coast, where the climate is warmer, there are mangrove swamps instead of salt marshes. The red mangrove is a small tree with long, curving roots growing out from its sides. The roots trap sediment to build up the land and provide shelter for countless fish and shellfish, which feed on the steady supply of falling mangrove leaves. Many of these animals are caught by fishermen.

A wide mangrove swamp is a coastline's best defense against the furious tropical storms called hurricanes, which stir the air into 100 mile per hour (160 kph) winds and send giant waves crashing against the coast. In the face of such violence, the mangroves, with their sturdy roots anchored securely in the soil, hold fast.

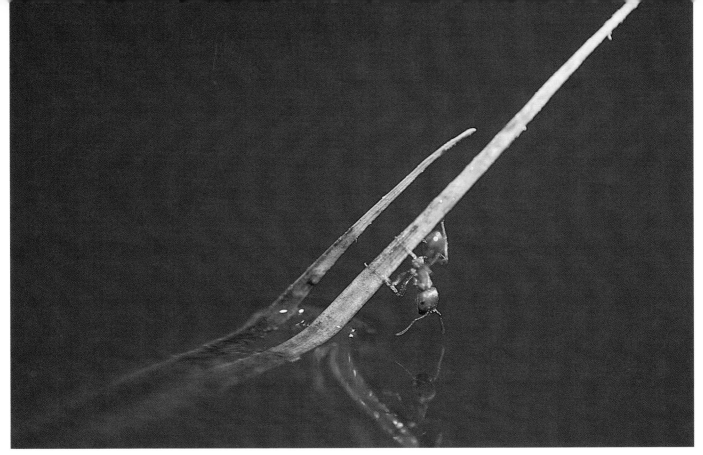
Insects help break down dead plants.

NATURE'S HIGH ENERGY FACTORIES

When a plant dies, there must be a way to recycle the nutrients in its body back into the environment. Otherwise they would all be used up, and there wouldn't be any nutrients left for future generations. Nutrient recycling begins when the dead plants are broken down by the process of decay, or **decomposition.** Decomposition is performed by decomposer organisms, especially the microscopic life forms called bacteria. Bacteria eat dead plants and animals and release nutrients back into the water and soil. Worms, insects, muskrats, and other creatures help the bacteria by chewing, tearing, and shredding the dead plants into smaller pieces.

Moving water speeds up nutrient recycling by mixing the pieces of plants and animals with the decomposer bacteria. Moving water also aids nutrient recycling by causing more water to contact the air and absorb oxygen. Decomposer organisms need plenty of oxygen.

Decomposition is especially fast in salt marshes and mangrove swamps, thanks to the constant movement of the tides. The mixture of brackish water, algae, and decaying plants is like a nutrient-rich milk shake. Fish, shrimp, snails, spiders, insects, and many other small creatures of the intertidal zone consume the material in this liquid. Some of these animals are the young of species caught by the fishermen of Louisiana and other coastal states.

A variety of birds, as well as muskrats, raccoons, otters, mice, sharks, and even an occasional dolphin may visit coastal wetlands to take advantage of the abundant food. The chain of large animals eating smaller animals that in turn eat plants is called the **food chain.** A food chain may have many steps or just a few steps. But no matter how many steps a food chain has, plants are always the first step. Wetlands are among the best places on earth for plants because of all the water and available nutrients there. Thus, wetlands support many food chains.

Fiddler crabs eat salt-marsh plants as the plants die.

Wetlands produce large numbers of plants, which provide food for all sorts of animals—even some crayfish, like the one at left.

Large numbers of plants are the reason biologists say wetlands have a high productivity. **Biological productivity** is the amount of plant material produced during a certain period of time. It is a measure of how fast plants grow. For example, the productivity of an average farm is about 2 pounds (0.9 kg) of new plant material on each square meter (1.2 square yards) of land during a year. A swamp forest in the southern United States, however, may produce twice that much. The productivity of a cattail marsh is even higher, and that of a salt marsh higher still. In fact, some salt marshes are as productive as dense South American rain forests. Habitats with high productivity can support many animals because there are lots of plants for them to eat.

A cypress swamp in Louisiana. The cypress is a common swamp tree.

When you look at a marsh or a swamp, it may not seem like there's that much new plant material being produced. That's because the plants grow fast and disappear soon after they die, as the decomposer organisms quickly dig into each new supply of dead plant material. While the decomposers are feasting, nutrients are being released. This cycle of death, decomposition, and nutrient return happens quickly beneath the water's surface, as long as the water has some movement. More plant life is produced and more plant life dies in a typical wetland than in almost any other kind of environment. As we'll see in the next chapter, however, there are some wetlands where productivity is low.

A baygall, a type of peat-forming wetland, in east Texas.

STORING ENERGY—THE PEATLANDS

As decomposer organisms break down the bodies of dead plants and animals in a wetland, much of the material produced settles to the bottom. There it combines with other sediments to form a type of soil called **muck**. You can't identify the kinds of plants muck came from because they have been decomposed so completely. Muck always looks like a dark, gooey mud, whether it sits at the bottom of a swamp or a marsh.

In some wetlands, however, the dead plants and animals aren't broken down much by decomposer organisms. Then, instead of forming muck, the slightly decomposed plant bodies form another type of soil called **peat**. If you know what to look for, you can tell what kinds of plants a section of peat came from because the plant bodies haven't decomposed much. Most wetlands contain some peat. But for a wetland to be classified as a **peatland**, the peat must be at least 16 inches (40 cm) deep.

As peaty soil builds up, both nutrients and energy are locked away with the dead plant material. With fewer nutrients and less energy available to them, plant growth is slower and the productivity is lower in a peatland than in either a swamp or a marsh.

Most of the peatlands in North America are called bogs. Bogs are common in Canada and the north-central and eastern United States. A bog often starts out as a lake that formed when rainwater and melting snow flowed into a low area. Unlike in an ordinary lake or marsh, there isn't any place for the water in a bog lake to run out. As a result, the water doesn't move, and it becomes **stagnant.** Stagnant water doesn't mix with the air and absorb oxygen the way moving water does. Decomposer bacteria need oxygen to do their jobs. Also, since bacteria can't swim around by themselves, they don't contact the pieces of dead plants and animals as often in stagnant water as they do in moving water.

Sphagnum moss, sometimes called peat moss, is the most common hydrophyte in most bogs.

PLANTS THAT EAT ANIMALS

Since bogs and fens have few nutrients for plant growth, some peatland plant species get their nutrients by eating animals. One of these meat-eating, or carnivorous, plants is the tiny sundew. If a small animal such as an ant steps on the sticky liquid covering the sundew's leaves, it may become trapped. The sundew then releases chemicals that break down the victim's body so that the plant can absorb the nutrients. The pitcher plant is another carnivorous species found in peat-forming wetlands. Its hollow leaf is shaped like a pitcher. If an insect enters the pitcher's leaf through an opening at the top, it can't leave because the inner leaf walls are too slippery to climb up. Soon, the unfortunate creature falls into a pool of liquid at the bottom of the leaf. Here its body is broken down and absorbed by the pitcher plant's cells.

This sundew is about to make a meal of an ant.

Decomposers also like warmth. But many bogs occur in the north, where the water remains cool even during the summer. Furthermore, bog plants often produce large amounts of acid. Acid can be useful to living things in small amounts, but a lot of acid can be harmful, especially for decomposer organisms. A bog's stagnant,

A fen, another type of peatland, in Colorado

acidic, oxygen-poor water results in a slow rate of decomposition and a rapid rate of peat formation.

Bogs may be less productive than marshes and swamps, but they still contain plenty of plants thanks to all the water. The most common hydrophyte in most bogs is sphagnum moss. It tolerates the difficult bog environment better than most other plants. As sphagnum moss dies, it becomes peat. Most of the peat in bogs comes from sphagnum moss, which is why peat is often called "peat moss."

Another kind of peatland is called a fen. Like bogs, fens produce peat. But the peat comes from a variety of reeds, sedges, and herbs that are very different from the plants in a bog. Also, unlike in a bog, the water in a fen is neither acidic nor stagnant. Fen water moves because it leaves the fen as a stream, but it moves slowly.

Even after a bog or fen is completely full of peat, it may still be a wetland with plenty of water. The water just isn't visible as it was before. Sphagnum peat can hold ten times its own weight in water. The ability of peat to hold large amounts of water is why people use it in gardens and flower pots. Peat is also valuable because the poorly decomposed plants of which it is formed still contain plenty of energy and nutrients. If the peat is dried out and burned as fuel, this energy is released as heat. In areas such as northern Europe, where there are lots of old bogs, peat is mined for use as a fuel to heat buildings. But sometimes peat miners find more than just peat. Since the peat in a bog doesn't decompose, anything that falls into the bog doesn't decompose either. Trees, animals, and even human bodies up to two thousand years old have been found perfectly preserved in peat deposits. The skin of the long-dead "bog people" has turned brown. But their hair, clothing, stomach contents, and sometimes even their facial expressions have changed little since their death.

A small wash flooding

KEEPERS OF THE LAND'S WATER

Another reason wetlands are valuable is that they protect us from floods. Swamps and marshes store the excess water from rain and melting snow, and release it slowly. Likewise, tremendous amounts of water sink into the sand and gravel of a wash before a stream ever appears on its surface. And when the water from a flooding river surges through the plants of a riparian floodplain, the current slows down and does less damage.

Wetlands may get some of their water from **groundwater.** Groundwater is water that drains down into soil and cracks in rocks, and collects underground. The highest level of the groundwater is called the **water table.** Many people get their drinking water from wells dug deep enough to reach the water table. Wetlands are often at the same level as the water table and may receive their water from springs where the groundwater flows out of the ground.

A scientist testing the water in a California marsh

But if a wetland lies above the water table, its water may sink down through the wetland's bottom and "recharge" the groundwater. If the groundwater is not recharged from time to time, it may run out. This would be a disaster for the millions of people who get their drinking water from groundwater. If the bottom of a wetland sits on top of clay, however, its water will not enter the groundwater, because clay particles are so close together that water cannot pass between them.

Wetlands don't just store water and release it slowly. They also keep it clean. As the particles of sediment settle on the bottom of a wetland, dangerous chemicals from mines, garbage dumps, factories, and towns may settle out with them. If there aren't too many of these substances, they may all become buried in the muck or peat and stay there forever, doing little harm. Some toxic substances are filtered out by floating hydrophytes, such as water hyacinths and duckweed. Wetlands also clean our water by removing some of the microscopic organisms that cause disease.

Chemicals from factories can pollute wetlands and threaten the wildlife that depends on them.

Some communities have saved millions of dollars by using wetlands to purify their drinking water instead of building costly water treatment plants. A few towns have actually flooded low areas and created marshes for water purification. These human-made wetlands are enjoyed by boaters and bird watchers, not to mention birds and other wildlife.

Of course, even the healthiest wetland may receive more harmful chemicals than it can handle and thus become polluted. The great marshy wildlife refuges in southern California have been poisoned by selenium, arsenic, and boron from fertilizers used on nearby farms. Rainwater runoff containing these deadly metals caused many of the refuges' ducklings to die before birth. Some of the dead had missing eyes. Others had deformed wings and beaks.

This floating house in a Louisiana bayou doesn't harm the natural environment.

NO NET LOSS

Because wetlands are so important in so many ways, many people in government are calling for "no net loss" of wetlands. This means that even if a wetland is destroyed, another should be created to take its place. But wetlands are so complex that creating one can be difficult. You may be able to cover a low area with water and then plant hydrophytes, but the wetland you've made may never have as many different kinds of plants and animals as a natural one. So it's important to protect each and every wetland we now have. Even the smallest wetlands help purify our drinking water, protect us from floods, and support large numbers of animals.

Unfortunately, many people don't realize how important wetlands are. "Too thick to drink and too thin to plow" is how wetlands are sometimes described. With all that water, you can't walk, drive, or build a house in most wetlands. Wetland plants often smell bad as they decompose. And some people don't know how to get along with certain wetland animals, such as snakes, alligators, and mosquitoes.

Riparian areas such as this cottonwood grove are popular places for people to live and play.

Saving our wetlands is also difficult because they often lie on privately owned land. Almost all the remaining prairie potholes and vernal pools in the United States are on private farms. Likewise, many valuable riparian areas sit beside rivers, washes, and streams that cross dozens of backyards and ranches.

A wetland's beauty can put it in danger too. This is especially true for riparian areas. A shady cottonwood grove is just the kind of place where someone might say, "This is where I want to build my house" or "start a farm" or "set up a town." And many people have done just that. There was never a lot of riparian land to begin with. Now most of it has been changed so much that it cannot be used by the animals that need it.

More and more wetlands are being taken over by businesses and homes.

When the United States first became a country, it had over two million acres of wetlands. About half of those are now gone. Some states have lost three-quarters or more of their original wetlands. California, Iowa, and Ohio have eliminated more than 90 percent. In Illinois, the wetland death toll stands at 99 percent.

Countless wetlands have been filled in and turned into oil refineries, airports, farms, factories, homes, and shopping centers. Miles of wetlands have also been dug out or dredged to make channels for boats. And some wetlands have dried up when their water was removed to fill swimming pools, sprinkle lawns, and water our food plants. Nowadays, with so many people in the world, the threat to wetlands is greater than ever. And the need to save our wetlands is greater than ever too, because there are so few left. No matter how much land we save in parks and wildlife refuges, if the wetlands that go with that land aren't saved too, the local animals won't have much of a chance.

Biologists say that because wetlands support so many different kinds of living things, their **biodiversity** is high. Lush tropical rain forests and colorful coral reefs are also biologically diverse habitats because, like wetlands, they contain a large variety of life forms.

Keeping the earth's biodiversity at its natural level is critical if we want to maintain the balance of nature, the relationship that all living things maintain with each other. Even if just one species of plant or animal disappears from an area, the balance will be tipped, and the biodiversity may fall. That's because other living things that depended on the lost species may disappear too.

Humans also suffer when biodiversity drops. The Louisiana fishermen found that out when their nets started coming up empty as the salt marshes disappeared. The men and women who hunt the ducks that breed in prairie potholes learned it too. And so did the children in a small New England town who listened for toads calling in the forest.

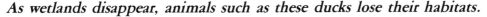

As wetlands disappear, animals such as these ducks lose their habitats.

GLOSSARY

biodiversity: the ability of an ecological system to support a wide variety of living things

biological productivity: the amount of living material produced in a given time period

decomposition: the breaking down of dead plants and animals, to release nutrients from their bodies

estuaries: parts of rivers where fresh river water mixes with salt water from the ocean

floodplains: low areas that are periodically flooded

food chain: a pattern of large animals eating smaller animals, which in turn eat plants. Plants are always at the bottom of a food chain.

groundwater: water that drains into the ground and is collected there

habitats: the places where a plant or animal normally lives

hydrophytes: water-loving plants that live in soil that is saturated at least for part of the year

mesophytes: plants that require moist but not saturated soil to live

muck: a dark, gooey type of soil made up of a mixture of sediments and fully decomposed plants and animals

mudflat: a flat area of mud that forms above the water's surface

peat: a type of soil that is made up of slightly decomposed plants and animals

peatland: a type of wetland in which the soil is peat that is at least 16 inches deep

rhizomes: plant stems that spread out underground and give rise to new plants

riparian areas: moist environments next to bodies of water

sediments: small solid particles that are carried by water or wind

stagnant: not moving or flowing

vernal pools: small temporary ponds that form in spring

water table: the highest level of groundwater

wet meadow: an edge of a marsh that is dry more often than it is wet and has different plants from the wetter part of the marsh

INDEX

algae, 13, 25, 27, 31
alligators, 14, 19, 42; "gator holes," 19
amphibians, 8, 10, 14

biodiversity, 45
biological productivity, 32–33
birds, 10, 14, 17, 19, 31
bogs, 9, 35, 36–37, 38
brackish water, 26, 31
bulrushes, 16

carnivorous plants, 36
cattails, 16, 18, 32
conserving wetlands, 42–44
creating wetlands, 42

decomposition, 30, 31, 33, 37, 38, 42;
    decomposer organisms, 30, 31, 34, 35, 36
deepwater environments, 11, 16
ducks, 7, 9, 41, 45

emergent plants, 16
estuaries, 26
Everglades National Park, 15

fens, 9, 37, 38
fishermen, 9, 29, 31, 45
fish, 9, 10, 17, 19, 29, 31; shellfish, 10, 27, 29,
    31
floating plants, 16, 40
floodplains, 22–23, 39
floods, 22–23, 39, 42
food chains, 31
forests, 8, 14, 22, 32
freshwater marshes, 9, 14, 16–18

grass, 7, 9, 14
groundwater, 39, 40

hydrophytes, 12–13, 14, 16, 20, 24, 25, 40, 42

insects, 30, 31, 36
intertidal zone, 24–25

lakes, 10, 20, 22, 35

mangroves, 29
marshes, 19, 22, 32, 33, 34, 35, 39

mesophytes, 20
muck, 34
mud, 13, 27, 34
mudflats, 9, 27, 28

nutrients, 23, 26, 30–31, 33, 38

oceans, 11, 13, 15, 26; coastal areas, 24

peat, 34–35, 37, 38
pollution, 40–41
ponds, 8, 9, 19, 21
prairie potholes, 7, 9, 16, 19, 43, 45
puddles, 11

raccoons, 14, 31
rain, 8, 15, 18, 19, 20, 21, 35, 41
reptiles, 10, 14, 17, 19
riparian areas, 9, 20, 22–23, 39, 43
rivers and streams, 10, 20, 22, 23, 26, 39, 43
rushes, 14

salt marshes, 9, 25, 26, 27–29, 45
salt water, 15, 24, 26
sedges, 14, 18, 37
snakes, 14, 17, 42
soil, 12, 20, 23; sediments, 23, 27, 28, 29, 40
spartina grass, 25, 27
sphagnum moss, 35, 37
stagnant water, 35, 36
submergent plants, 16
swamps, 9, 14, 15, 22, 32, 33, 34, 39; mangrove
    swamps, 29

tides, 24, 26, 27, 28
toads, 8, 9, 19, 45

vernal pools, 9, 21, 43

washes, 9, 20, 39, 43
water purification, 40–41, 42
water table, 39–40
wetlands, definition of, 11
wet meadows, 9, 18, 19
wildlife refuges, 41, 44

ABOUT THE AUTHOR

Frank Staub is the author of several books for children, including *Yellowstone's Cycle of Fire* and *America's Prairies,* both published by Carolrhoda Books. He has also written dozens of magazine articles and created numerous film strips and slide sets. Staub holds degrees in Biology and Zoology. He works as a freelance writer and photographer, which allows him to travel and study the places and events that interest him most. When he's not working, he climbs mountains and enjoys sea kayaking, bicycling, and skin diving.